THE EYES OF A WISH

THE EYES OF A WISH

A PHOTOGRAPHIC AND LITERARY CELEBRATION OF THE CHILDREN, FAMILIES, AND VOLUNTEERS OF THE MAKE-A-WISH FOUNDATION®

Edited by Preston Merchant

Produced by J. Wade Caldwell

With a Foreword by Kevin Sharp

Make-A-Wish Foundation® of America

THE MAKE-A-WISH® STORY

In 1980, a 7-year-old Phoenix, Arizona, boy with leukemia wanted to be a police officer. Officers from the Arizona Department of Public Safety granted his wish with a custom-made uniform, helmet, badge and even a helicopter ride! That child's delight in having his wish come true inspired a group of volunteers to form the first Make-A-Wish Foundation® chapter.

How is the organization structured? Although the first chapter started in 1980, the Make-A-Wish Foundation® of America was created in 1983 to oversee the growth and development of the organization and establish consistent policies and guidelines. Since 1983, the national organization has evolved into a central service office that provides a myriad of services to the chapters, including financial assistance, training, fund raising, marketing support, and policy/governance.

Today, the Make-A-Wish Foundation® has 82 chapters throughout the United States, Puerto Rico, Guam, and the District of Columbia. Nationally, almost 82% of all money donated goes directly to granting wishes to the children, with the balance divided between administration and fundraising. These percentages earned the Foundation an "A" rating from the leading journal on philanthropy. Call 800.722.9474 to find the chapter located in your area or go to www.wish.org for more information.

WHAT IS MAKE-A-WISH®?

The Make-A-Wish Foundation® is the largest and most respected wish-granting organization in the world. It exists for one purpose: to fulfill the special wishes of children under the age of 18 who have life-threatening illnesses.

The foundation is a non-profit, privately funded organization composed of almost 13,000 volunteers in 82 chapters in the United States and its territories. In addition, Make-A-Wish Foundation® International has 13 affiliates in other nations.

In the year ending August 31, 1997, Make-A-Wish® volunteers in the United States granted 7,041 wishes. At the same time, volunteers of Make-A-Wish® International fulfilled more than 800 additional wishes. Volunteers in the Unites States have fulfilled more than 50,000 wishes since the first Make-A-Wish® chapter was founded in 1980.

FOREWORD

BY KEVIN SHARP

NASHVILLE RECORDING ARTIST & WISH KID

I was angry, I was scared, and I wondered why me? I was facing almost certain death due to bone cancer that spread from my leg to my lungs. In the midst of this unbelievably difficult time, a ray of light, of hope, came shining through. Words cannot fully describe the impact of my wish—to meet one of my musical heroes, David Foster, the producer and performer of many of my favorite songs.

Since music has always been an integral part of my life, I can say that the joy and inspiration from having that wish granted were overwhelming. David became a friend and advocate, helping me start a career in music.

The smile on my face from that day is still with me now. To know that some 50,000 kids have had the opportunity to smile as I did brings a special warmth to my heart. The common thread that unites us as wish kids can truly be seen in *The Eyes of a Wish.*™

I thank all of you who have made so many dreams come true for so many kids. Thanks Make-A-Wish® Let's keep up the great work.

THE PRODUCTION OF THIS BOOK WAS POSSIBLE ONLY THROUGH THE GENEROUS SUPPORT
OF THE FOLLOWING UNDERWRITERS:

6}10 STUDIO, INC.

AGFA DIVISION, BAYER CORPORATION

BAY NETWORKS

DUN & BRADSTREET FOUNDATION

FOCUS ATLANTA

NETSCAPE COMMUNICATIONS CORPORATION

VIRTUAL RESOURCES, INC.

THE SUPPORT OF THE UNDERWRITERS AND THE CONTRIBUTIONS OF THOSE LISTED BELOW
HAVE MADE IT POSSIBLE FOR ALL OF THE PROCEEDS FROM THE SALE OF THIS BOOK
TO GO DIRECTLY TO MAKE-A-WISH FOUNDATION® OF GREATER ATLANTA & NORTH GEORGIA

THE THOUGHTS AND IMAGES EXPRESSED IN THE EYES OF A WISH™
ARE THE PRODUCT OF A GROUP OF CARING AND CREATIVE VOLUNTEERS
WHO BELIEVE IN THE WONDERFUL WORK MAKE-A-WISH FOUNDATION® DOES.

PRESTON MERCHANT
Editor

J. WADE CALDWELL
Concept   Design   Production

PROJECT ADVISORY COMMITTEE
Jim Grant   Wendy Roberts   Tony DeMartino

MAKE-A-WISH FOUNDATION® OF GREATER ATLANTA & NORTH GEORGIA
Diane Valek, Executive Director
Stephanie Nelson, Director, Communications & Special Events   Helen M. Shepard, Director, Program Services

CONTRIBUTORS

DIANA AGAN
photographer

LINDA AMMONS
writer

J. WADE CALDWELL
photographer

LIAN DAVIS CHAPMAN
photographer

JOHN DAUBLE
photographer

NATHAN FEDER
photographer

GAIL GIORGIO
writer

LAURA HELMS
writer

TOI B. JAMES
writer

PAM McKNIGHT
wish mom & writer

JETAIME PILON
photographer

W. PATRICK QUEEN
wish dad & writer

HELEN M. SHEPARD
photographer

SANDRA WARREN
wish mom & photographer

LINDA WINN
photographer

INTRODUCTION

BY J. WADE CALDWELL

Someone once said that inspiration descends in flashes. The inspiration for *The Eyes of a Wish*™ can be traced to one moment while helping make a wish come true—the first time I saw Kristen. Her eyes reached out and planted a seed that will grow for many years to come. It is only through that brief flash and the unwavering support of Kristen's family that this book was possible.

Several weeks after that visit, with the vision of the book taking shape, I returned to take the first photos of Kristen. Looking through the lens, I saw many expressions with which I would become very familiar as I took photographs of the children. I saw what having a wish granted meant to these children. From visits with Mickey and celebrities to computers and travel—the wishes varied but the emotion in their eyes, when asked about their wish, never did.

When this project was conceived, there were three goals I wanted to achieve: 1) to involve a wide range of volunteers, including writers, photographers, and coordinators, in creating a lasting celebration of the children of Make-A-Wish®; 2) to raise funds through the sale of the book that would contribute to the granting of future wishes; and 3) to increase the level of volunteer support and community awareness of the Make-A-Wish Foundation.® The result of the first goal you hold in your hands. In order for the other two goals to be achieved, *The Eyes of a Wish*™ must inspire you to get involved.

It is my most sincere wish that you will see that flash of inspiration somewhere among the eyes, the smiles, and the words that celebrate the spirit and joy of the these incredible children. There is nothing easy about volunteering, making a donation, or telling a friend about Make-A-Wish.® There is also nothing as rewarding as looking into the eyes of a wish. You can make a difference.

I dedicate this book to Kristen for showing me what is important
and
to my parents for setting an example of how to give to others.

Make-A-Wish Foundation® of America

800.722.WISH (9474) 602.279.WISH   fax 602.279.0855

100 West Clarendon, Suite 2200, Phoenix, AZ 85013-3518

www.wish.org

The Make-A-Wish Foundation® has independent chapters across the United States. This Chapter Listing shows where chapters are located. If you have any questions or want to know how you can support the chapter in your area, please call 1.800.722.WISH (9474) or visit our web site at www.wish.org for more information.

ALABAMA
MAWF of Alabama

ARIZONA
MAWF of Central & Southern Arizona
MAWF of Northern Arizona

ARKANSAS
See Tennessee – MAWF of the Mid-South
(covers entire state of Arkansas)

CALIFORNIA
Greater Bay Area MAWF
MAWF of Los Angeles
MAWF of Orange County
MAWF of South San Joaquin Valley
MAWF of Sacramento
MAWF of San Diego
MAWF of the Tri-Counties

COLORADO
MAWF of Colorado

CONNECTICUT
MAWF of Connecticut

DELAWARE
See Maryland – MAWF of the Mid-Atlantic
(covers entire state of Delaware)

DISTRICT OF COLUMBIA
See Maryland – MAWF of the Mid-Atlantic
(covers the District of Columbia)

FLORIDA
MAWF of Central Florida
MAWF of Sarasota/Tampa Bay
MAWF of South Florida

GEORGIA
MAWF of Central & Southern Georgia
MAWF of Greater Atlanta & North Georgia

GUAM
MAWF of Guam

HAWAII
MAWF of Hawaii

IDAHO
MAWF of Idaho

ILLINOIS
MAWF of Central Illinois
MAWF of Northern Illinois
Southern Illinois
See Missouri – MAWF of Metro St. Louis

INDIANA
MAWF of Indiana

IOWA
MAWF of Iowa

KANSAS
MAWF of Kansas

LOUISIANA
MAWF of Louisiana

MAINE
MAWF of Maine

MARYLAND
MAWF of the Mid-Atlantic

MASSACHUSETTS
MAWF of Greater Boston
MAWF of Central & Western Massachusetts

Kristen

THE EYES OF A WISH

Making a Wish

Not more than six or seven years old,

she had the aura of a guru

with eyes

that could tell a thousand stories

of pain and happiness.

Still,

her giggle

quickly reminded me

that she was merely a baby

who needed guidance and love.

How ironic it is to meet a child

who could teach you,

as an adult,

to grow up

and to live life to the fullest

— with just a glance.

an excerpt from an essay by Toi B. James

STEPHANIE - II
COMPUTER

Wade Caldwell

A LITTLE SOMETHIN'

ADEBOYIN - 15
WALT DISNEY WORLD RESORT®

Wade Caldwell

Robin Davidson, wish volunteer

I'm just a little man,
With a big plan,
To make your day.

Enjoying peek-a-boo,
Finding you-know-who,
The games I could play.

➤

NATOSHA "SHEA" - 4
WALT DISNEY WORLD RESORT®

Wade Caldwell

BRIAN - 12
COMPUTER

Wade Caldwell

Listen to ocean seas,

Feel the soft, gentle breeze,

As I sit and ponder.

Hold my hand,

Take a stand,

Allowing wishful thoughts to wander.

➤

BRITTANY - 8
COMPUTER

Linda Winn & Diana Agan

RYAN - 7
WALT DISNEY WORLD RESORT®

So much to do
And share with you,
Time well deserved.

Innocent eyes,
No good-byes,
Precious moments to preserve.

by Toi B. James

ADEBOYIN - 15
WALT DISNEY WORLD RESORT®

Adeboyin's father Francis   Wade Caldwell

MICHAEL - 4
WALT DISNEY WORLD RESORT®

Wade Caldwell

FUTURE PLANS

A doctor,

A lawyer,

A pilot,

A saint.

Dream the impossible dream,

The next Mona Lisa I may paint.

NATOSHA "SHEA" - 4
WALT DISNEY WORLD RESORT®

Wade Caldwell

Helen Shepard   Christy Whitney, wish volunteer

A policeman,

An oceanographer,

A fireman,

A photographer.

Good times and bad times I share,

All bearable with a little tender-loving care.

➣

MICHAEL - 4
WALT DISNEY WORLD RESORT®

Scott Westmorelend, volunteer

Wade Caldwell

MASON - 4
WALT DISNEY WORLD RESORT®

Wade Caldwell   Jan Moses, wish volunteer

A preacher,

A teacher,

A guru,

The Pope.

Changing the world with a simple thought,
Anything is possible with love, wisdom, and hope.

by Toi B. James

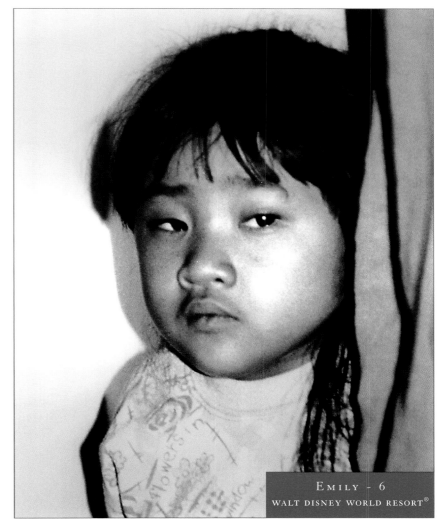

EMILY - 6
WALT DISNEY WORLD RESORT®

LiAn Chapman

THE ONE AND ONLY MOUSE

JUSTIN - 9
TV/VCR

Wade Caldwell

He's the one and only mouse
Mama ever lets into our house . . .

His large round perky ears
Hear my awful-awfullest fears.

When I ride my bike a thousand miles,
He rides along with open smiles.

Although Donald is his true-blue pal,
And Minnie is probably his special gal,

And Goofy is someone he's silly around,
I'm the best friend Mickey's found.

Unlike Pluto who probably can bark,
Mickey's not scared of the darkest-dark.
➤

CODY - 6
WALT DISNEY WORLD RESORT®

Linda Winn & Diana Agan

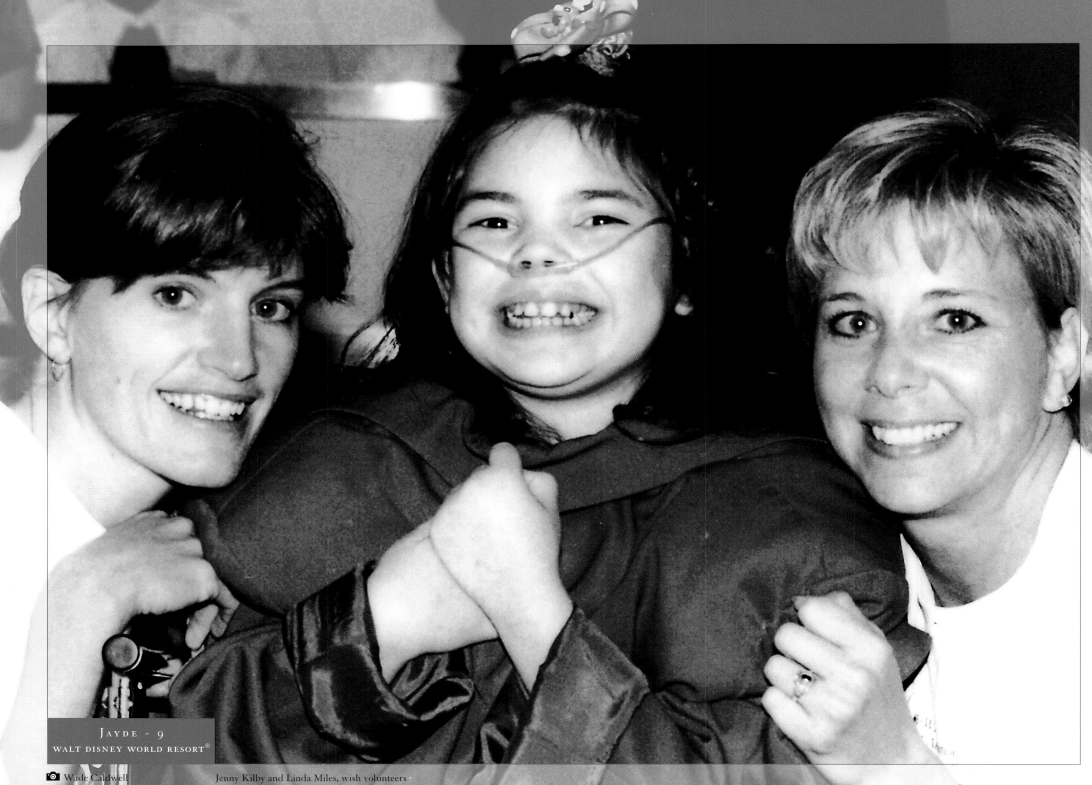

JAYDE - 9
WALT DISNEY WORLD RESORT®

Wade Caldwell   Jenny Kilby and Linda Miles, wish volunteers

He's not afraid to hug me awake
And never complains about the noise I make.

With his hand squeezed tight in mine,
I know that things soon'll be fine.

I know he's truly my truest friend,
One who'll be there at every bend.

One who'll pretend whenever I play,
One who'll be there at the end of the day.

Yes, Mickey's allowed into our house
Because he's no screechy-pesty mouse.

by Gail Giorgio

TYLER - 5
WALT DISNEY WORLD RESORT®

John Dauble

THE BRUSH OF ANGELS' WINGS

LARRY - 17
COMPUTER

Wade Caldwell

God has plans for this child, one of

His wondrous works of art.

He will always protect and guide,

and the angels will never depart.

an excerpt from a poem by Sarah's Grandmother, Bertie Spradlin

BETH - 14
COMPUTER

Linda Winn & Diana Agan

TYRONE - 10
TO BE AN ACTOR

LiAn Chapman   Helen Shepard, staff

AND THE BEAT GOES ON . . .

Days rush by,

Evenings fall and dwell,

Moments wave and sigh,

Seconds tick the time to tell.

Music fills the air,

Notes dance on my heels,

Not a minute to spare,

While melodies cover the fields.

I sing . . .

KAITLYN - 4
WALT DISNEY WORLD RESORT®

Helen Shepard

CARYN - 13
TO PLAY THE PIANO

pianist Jean-Yves Thibaudet

I am Woman,

Hear me roar.

With a coy smile . . .

I am Eagle,

See me soar.

No questions asked,

No time to waste,

Promises to cash,

No room for haste.

➤

KRISTEN · 3
ROOM REDECORATION

Wade Caldwell

DANA - 16
VISIT NEW YORK CITY

📷 Wade Caldwell

Life moves fast,

Like a Gershwin tune,

Stepping with a dash,

Not a thought too soon.

Enjoying all pleasures,

With God's gifts at hand,

Schedule music sessions,

All part of the life I plan.

And the beat goes on . . .

by Toi B. James

KATE - 15

Tammy McCurley, wish volunteer

Jetaime Pilon

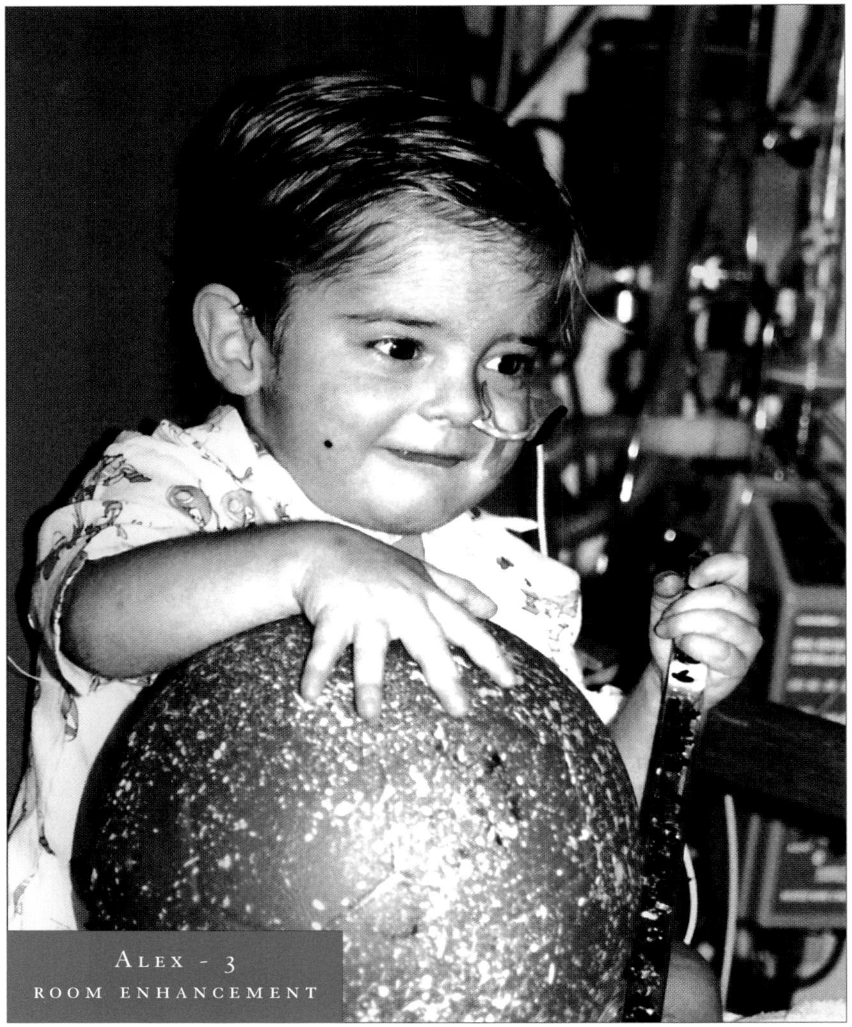

BEACH WISHES

ALEX - 3
ROOM ENHANCEMENT

Wade Caldwell

Sun hanging low, bouncing down

Red-orange-round like the nose of a clown

Sea dark and far where the red nose sinks

Sky overhead candy-bubble-gum-pink

➢

make a wish!

Jordache

STACEY - 9
WALT DISNEY WORLD RESORT®

Lisa LoBuglio, wish volunteer   Wade Caldwell

Squishy-scratch sand between pruny-wet toes

Wrapping up warm in nighty-time clothes

Glowy-gray coals that match the sun

Burgers and dogs in soggy-sog buns

➤

TYRONE - 10
TO BE AN ACTOR

LiAn Chapman

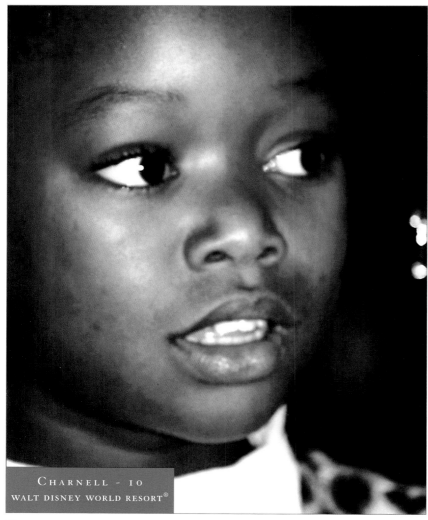

CHARNELL - 10
WALT DISNEY WORLD RESORT®

Wade Caldwell

Hop-hopping back over sharpy-smooth shells

Dropping the pieces in the wishing well

Feet on white lines step-step to the car

Beach wishes float high, each reaching its star

by Laura Helms

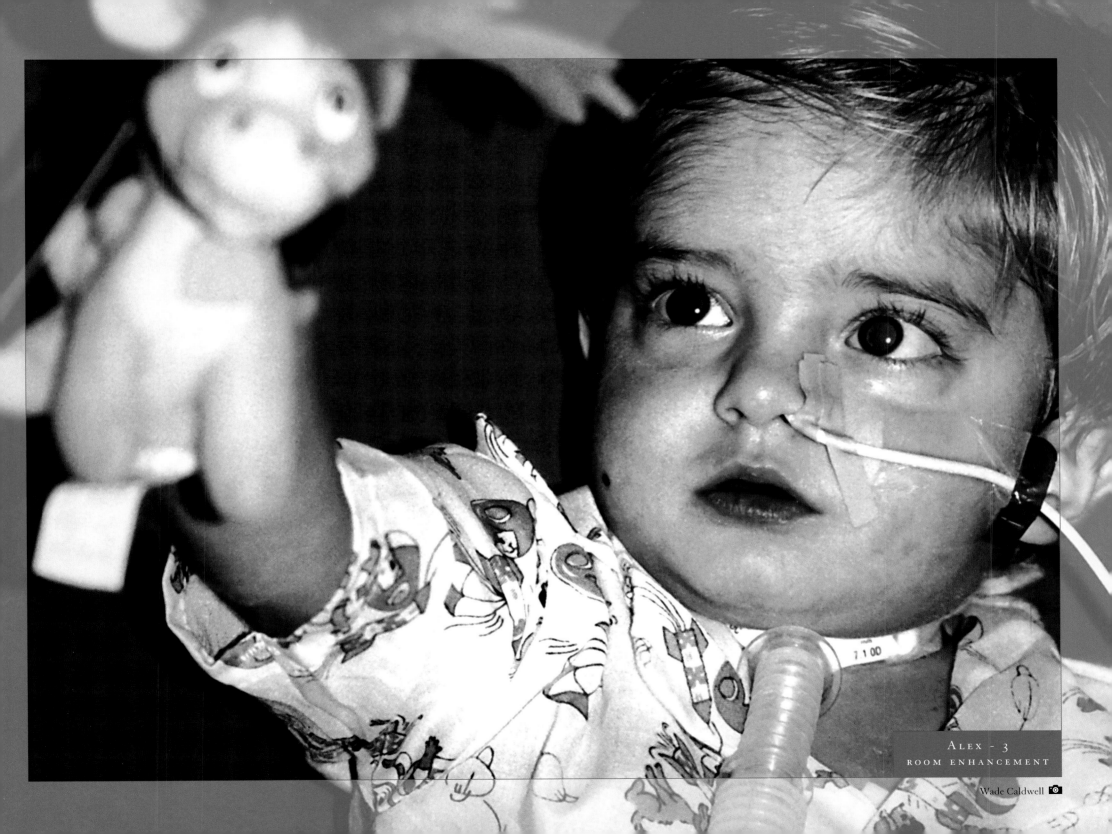

ALEX - 3
ROOM ENHANCEMENT

Wade Caldwell

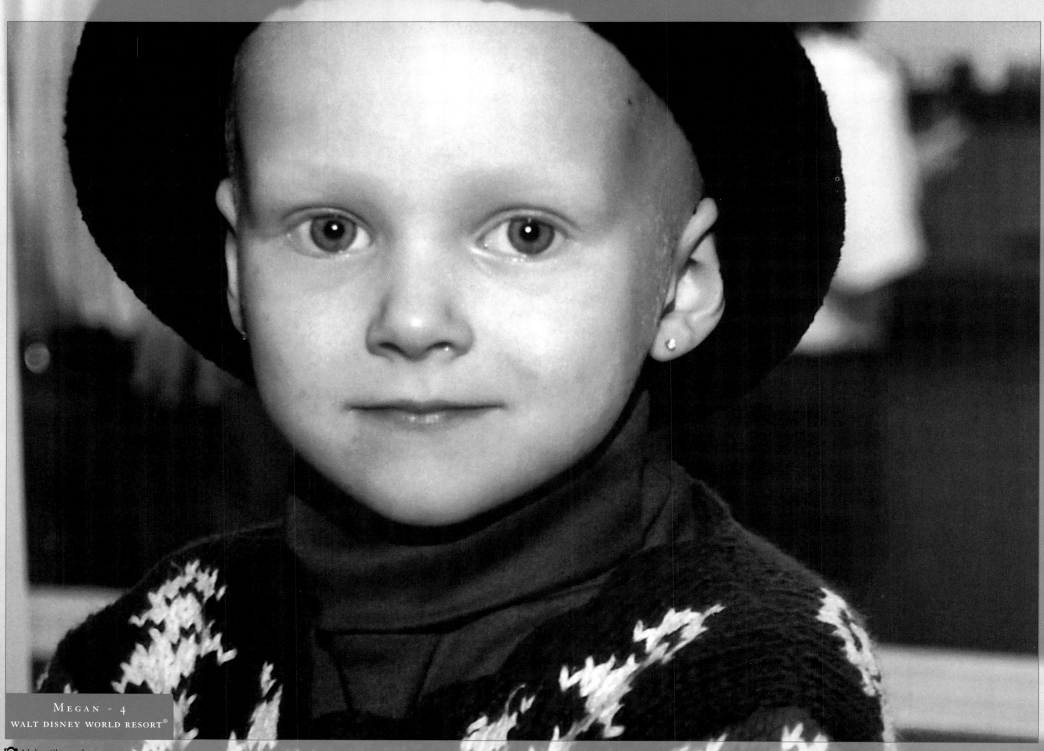

MEGAN - 4
WALT DISNEY WORLD RESORT®

Helen Shepard

Pennies and Clothes Pins

He's growing up,

That tiny little worm.

With the huge blue eyes,

And pixie smile.

He's growing up and away.

The little legs that used

To struggle with the tricycle

Can balance and ride a two-wheeled bike.

No training wheels.

➤

JEREMY - 6
WALT DISNEY WORLD RESORT®

Wade Caldwell 📷

CARYN - 13
TO PLAY THE PIANO

　　　　　Atlanta Symphony Orchestra President, Allison Vulgamore

There is that sense of pride and emptiness

As my youngest child grows up.

Until now, he has been my baby.

But he's up and away, pockets full

Of pennies and clothes pins.

Camping and fishing with dad,

Bike riding with big brother.

More and more time he spends with them.

And at the age of four,

Kisses for mom are rationed out,

Until I hunger for them.

➤

KAITLYN - 4
WALT DISNEY WORLD RESORT®

Helen Shepard

SHOLANDA - 11
PINK PLAYHOUSE

LESARA - 9
WALT DISNEY WORLD RESORT®

Helen Shepard   Sholanda and LeSara's mother Yolanda

But just when I think

That I've finally lost,

A tiny little body, clad in a thick

blanket sleeper, will cuddle beside me

in bed, put his arms around my neck and

whisper sweet, sweet words:

I love you, my mommy.

by Linda Ammons

WALLACE - 4
WALT DISNEY WORLD RESORT®

Wallace's mom Angela   Helen Shepard 📷

JOSHUA - 4
WALT DISNEY WORLD RESORT®

Wade Caldwell

Amanda & Shawn (r)

Heidi · 15
VISIT HAWAII

Christy Whitney, wish volunteer

Helen Shepard

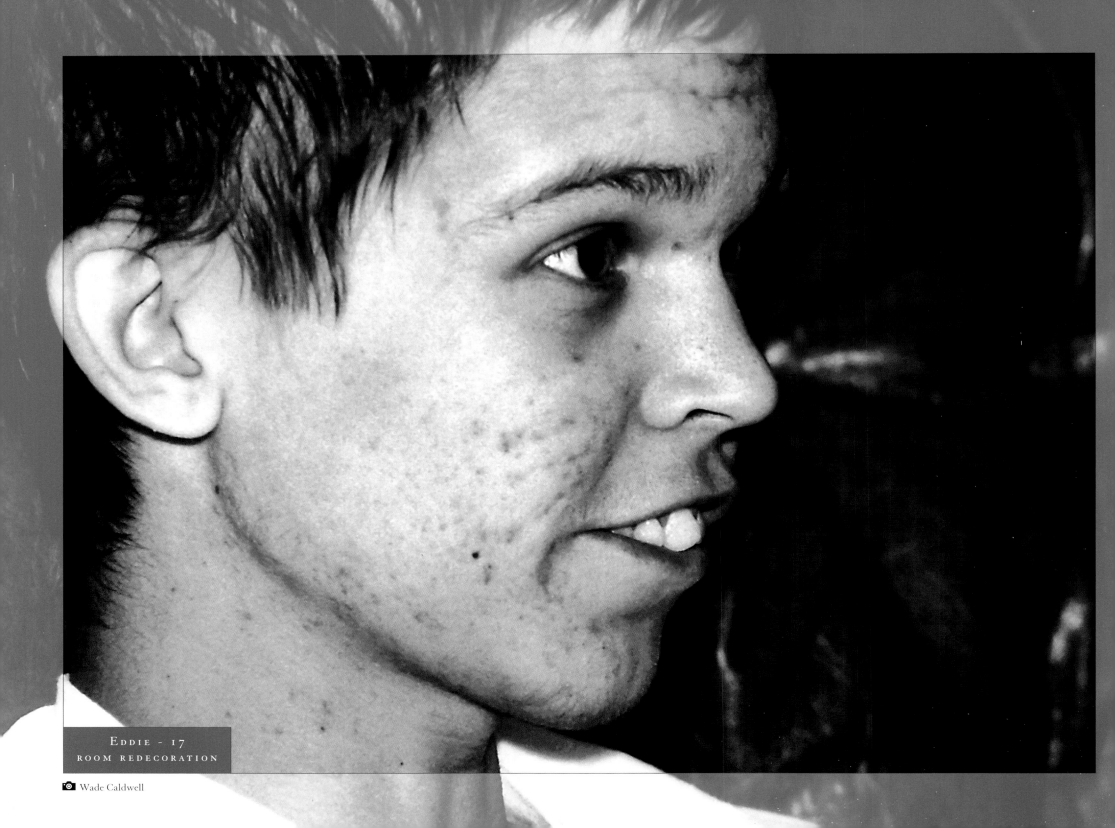

EDDIE - 17
ROOM REDECORATION

Wade Caldwell

THE BRUSH OF ANGELS' WINGS

This small and most precious child

has taught us so many things . . .

that I'm not surprised to hear

the brush of angels' wings . . .

In Sarah's presence.

an excerpt from a poem by Sarah's Grandmother, Bertie Spradlin

VICTORIA - 4
WALT DISNEY WORLD RESORT®

Wade Caldwell

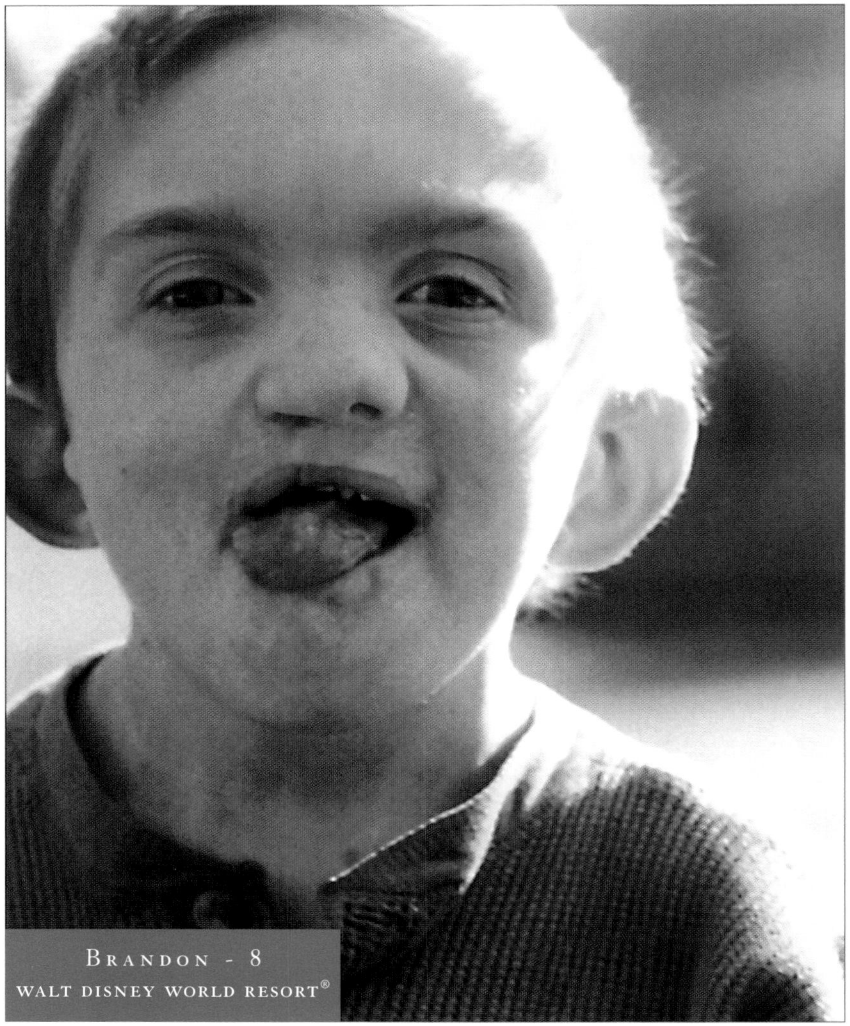

Learn with Me

Mommy . . . Mommy . . .

Look what I can do.

I can . . .

Touch the sky,

Walk the moon,

Sing a song,

Grab a spoon!

➤

TYLER - 4
WALT DISNEY WORLD RESORT®

Tyler's mom Jina   John Dauble

VICTORIA - 4
WALT DISNEY WORLD RESORT®

Jetaime Pilon   Jeremy McNeely, wish volunteer

See me . . .

Hug the clouds,
Embrace the rain,
Love the earth,
It's not the same!

➤

JUAN - 10
BIG RED BOAT CRUISE

Sloane Thompson, wish volunteer

Wade Caldwell

EDDIE - 17
ROOM ENHANCEMENT

Wade Caldwell

Show me how to . . .

Make people see:
Life is great,
That's the plan,
For goodness sake!
Don't you want to learn with me?

by Toi B. James

{48}

BRITTANY - 8
COMPUTER

Brittany's mom Cindy   Linda Winn & Diana Agan

Nathan Feder   Caryn's father Joseph

DADDY, DADDY

Daddy, Daddy, please don't cry.
I know I look tired and weak,
But you must listen when I speak
And wipe the tears from your eye.

Daddy, Daddy, please don't cry.
I know you don't really understand,
But stay by me and hold my hand
And I promise I won't die.

Daddy, Daddy, please don't cry.
I'm not well, but I'm getting better.
I'll follow their instructions to the letter.
I'll try not to ask why.

➢

DANA - 16
VISIT NEW YORK CITY

fellow band member Jeremy Cruise Wade Caldwell

MASON - 4
WALT DISNEY WORLD RESORT®

Wade Caldwell, volunteer

Daddy, Daddy, please don't cry.
The pain is not really so bad.
I hate to see you look so sad;
You must promise me that you'll try!

Daddy, Daddy, it's okay to cry.
I know you're trying to be brave.
But don't worry, my life we'll save.
Together, we'll reach for the sky!

by W. Patrick Queen, Alyson's father
from his book Bent . . . But Not Broken

ALYSON - 6
WALT DISNEY WORLD RESORT®

Wade Caldwell

BRITTANY - 8
WALT DISNEY WORLD RESORT®

Wade Caldwell

WHATEVER

I look forward to all life's mysteries,
Whatever they may be.

Rivers meeting fellow waters
As they challenge the sea.

Sunsets with rays of fire,
Moonlight beams with stars sitting higher.

Whatever the fact,
Wherever the chatter,

Don't ever forget,
Small things matter.

STARGUAR "TRE" - 7
COMPUTER

Marie Mize, wish volunteer

Jetaime Pilon

BETH - 14
COMPUTER

Beyond the laughter and schemes,
I blindly see you.

Above the tears and the pain,
I thankfully love, too.

Whatever stories will be told,
Wishful thoughts I shall always hold.

by Toi B. James

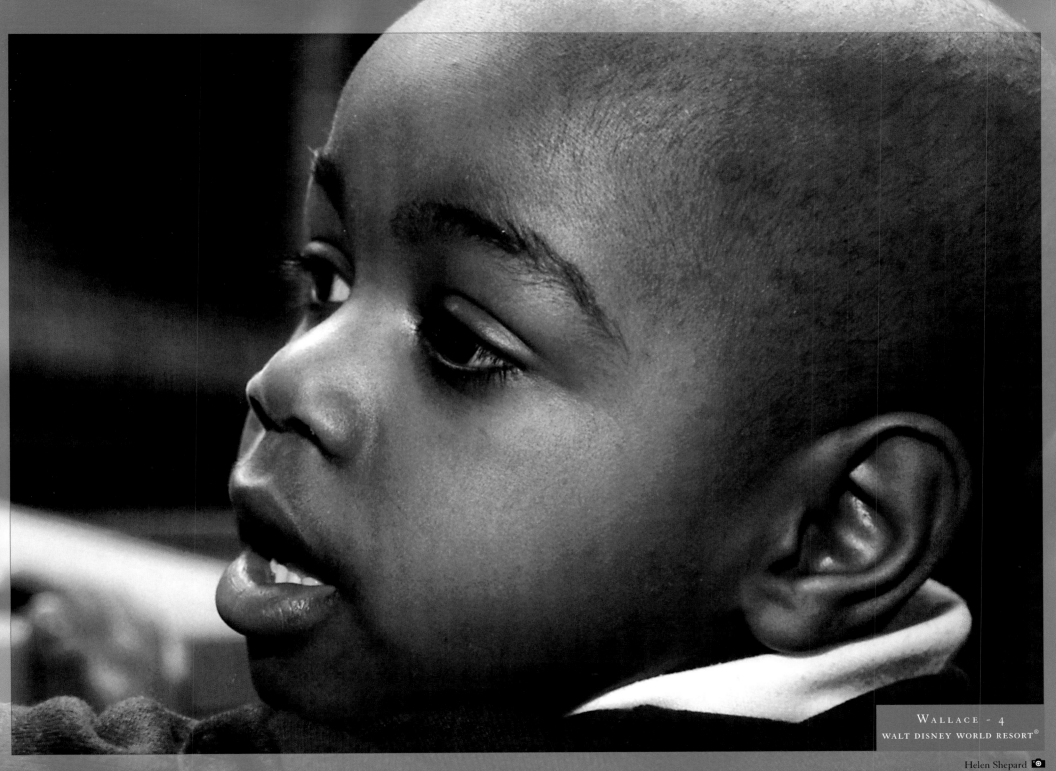

WALLACE - 4
WALT DISNEY WORLD RESORT®

Helen Shepard

ERIN - 8
PUPPY

Linda Winn & Diana Agan

FRIEND OR FOE?

He's always with me. I know he's my friend,

And together we'll fight to the bitter end;

'Cause my buddy's beside me through thick and thin.

We will fight this cancer and

We will win!

an excerpt from a poem by W. Patrick Queen

from his book Bent . . . But Not Broken

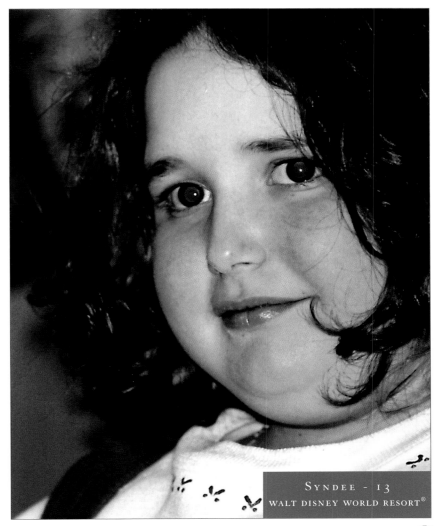

SYNDEE - 13
WALT DISNEY WORLD RESORT®

Wade Caldwell

THE EYES OF CHILDREN

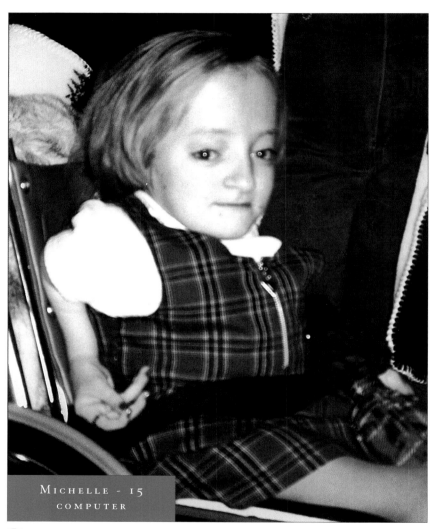

MICHELLE - 15
COMPUTER

LiAn Chapman

A child's eyes are filled with love

just like a newborn dove.

As the sun rises over the valley

with the innocence of the new day,

I look into those twinkling eyes

and never see the tragedy.

I only see how love replies.

To love a child means everything to me –

to watch the dove flap its wings and fly free.

by Pam McKnight, Bryan's mother

BRYAN - 8
WALT DISNEY WORLD RESORT®

LiAn Chapman

ERIC - 17
ENTERTAINMENT CENTER

Wade Caldwell

Night Rainbow

As a child I gazed in awe
At rainbows formed from
Sunshine and rain fragments.
God made rainbows, someone said,
As a promise to His children
To never destroy the earth.
I took this at face value.

As an adult, I forgot to see
The rainbows in the clouds,
Seeing instead the utter
Destruction in my life.
Where are the rainbows?
Where are the promises?
And what about my life?

➤

Brittany- 8
WALT DISNEY WORLD RESORT®

Wade Caldwell

TERESA - II
TV/VCR

Wade Caldwell

As a mother, I saw rainbows
Through the innocent eyes
Of my young and curious children.
God made rainbows, I told them,
As a promise to His children
To never destroy the earth.
They took this at face value.

Tonight, I sat beneath a
Newly washed sky and saw the
Moon, in all its glory, full
And encircled by a huge ring,
Wive's tales say that means rain,
I laugh softly.
It's been raining all day.

➤

Syndee's family: Michael, Arlene, and Brett

Wade Caldwell

STEPHANIE- 11
COMPUTER

Wade Caldwell

But just inside the circle,

Directly around the light of the moon,

Is a circle of colors: Night Rainbow.

"I made rainbows," the quiet voice said,

"As a promise to you,

To never destroy the earth."

I suddenly knew that He wouldn't.

by Linda Ammons

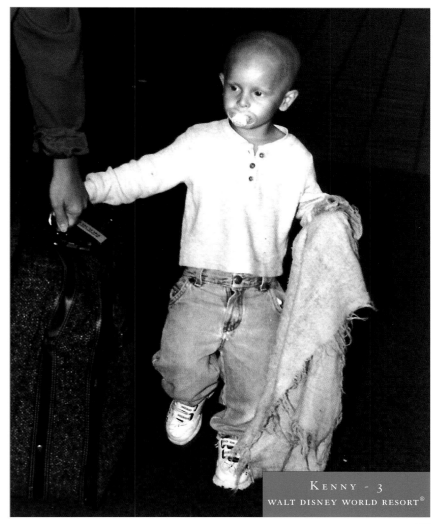

KENNY - 3
WALT DISNEY WORLD RESORT®

Wade Caldwell

SHOLANDA - II
PINK PLAYHOUSE

Wade Caldwell

JUAN - 10
BIG RED BOAT CRUISE

Wade Caldwell

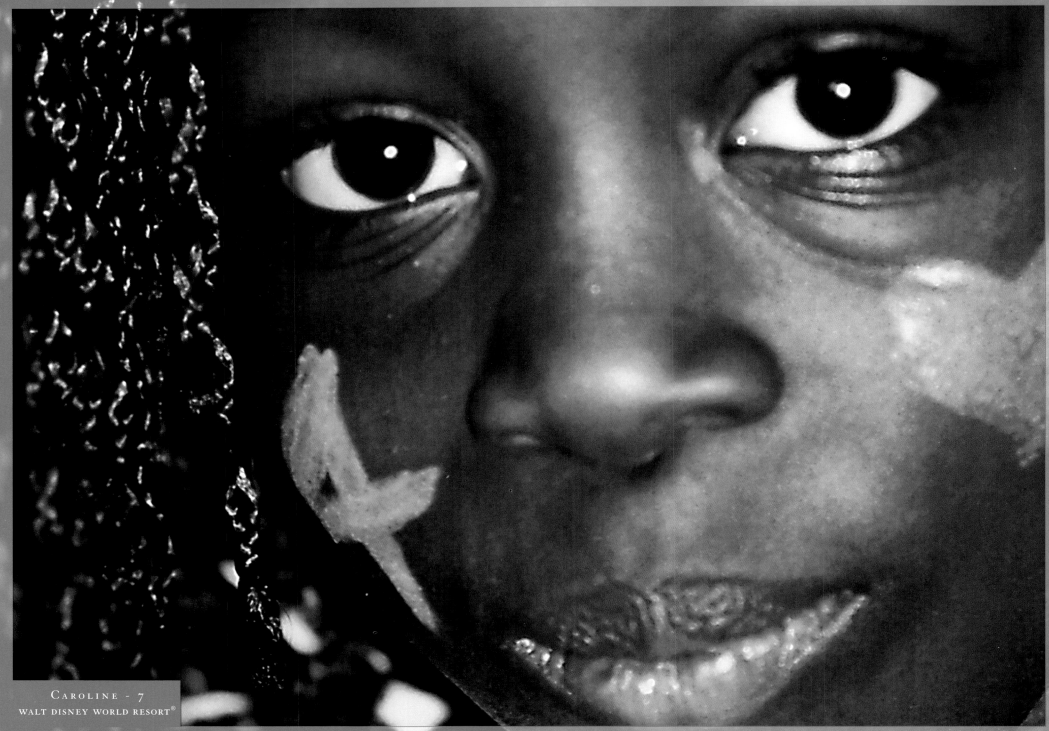

CAROLINE - 7
WALT DISNEY WORLD RESORT®

FRIENDS FOREVER

I have a special blanket
That's forever always mine.
It doesn't steal my toys,
And it doesn't ever whine.

Before my mama bore me,
My blanket flew down here,
A snuggly guardian angel
Who whispered in my ear.

KENNY · 3
WALT DISNEY WORLD RESORT®

Helen Shepard, staff, and Ken, Kyle, and Laura   Wade Caldwell

JARRATT- 10
WALT DISNEY WORLD RESORT®

Wade Caldwell

Scott Westmoreland, volunteer

It said, "You're very special,
I'll keep you safe and warm,
I'll be your friend forever,
As I snuggle 'round your arm."

➢

Outside it's badly tattered.

Inside its threads are new.

It's always here beside me

Especially when I'm blue.

➤

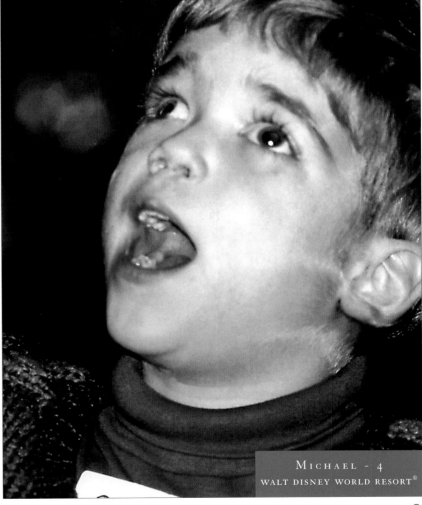

MICHAEL - 4
WALT DISNEY WORLD RESORT®

Wade Caldwell 📷

Lori Brown, wish volunteer

It chases away the scaries
And the monsters in my room.
It's close to give me cover
From wherever monsters loom.

It rests upon my pillow
When I fall asleep each night.
And always in the morning
It's here to greet the light.

➤

CHAD - 12
ENTERTAINMENT CENTER

Wade Caldwell

CHRISTY - 5
WALT DISNEY WORLD RESORT®

Wade Caldwell   Christy's father Edward

While lassoing wild horses,

My blanket's in my hand,

Always there to pad me

When on the moon I land.

Lost for sure a time or two,

A sad sack all alone,

By magic it turned up

In someone else's home.

JAYDE - 9
WALT DISNEY WORLD RESORT®

Wade Caldwell

JACQUELINE - 5
WALT DISNEY WORLD RESORT®

LiAn Chapman

No better bestest friend
Could any person clutch
Than a special huggly blanket
That cares so very much.

No matter where I travel,
No matter where I roam,
My snuggly angel blanket
Will safely guide me home.

by Gail Giorgio

HELLO
my name is

Janiqua

JANIQUA - 3
WALT DISNEY WORLD RESORT®

Wade Caldwell

JASON - 8
MEET THE BRAVES

Wade Caldwell

GRANTED

A hug,

A smile,

A tear,

A hand,

Treasures that all can give.

➤

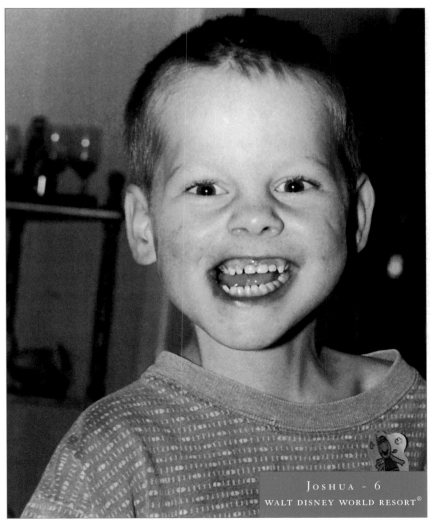

JOSHUA - 6
WALT DISNEY WORLD RESORT®

Wade Caldwell 📷

Wade Caldwell

To share,

To give,

To love,

A friend,

Gifts that can help a child to live.

by Toi B. James

COLBI - 6
COMPUTER

Helen Shepard

EPILOGUE

BY PRESTON MERCHANT

Until recently, I thought of Make-A-Wish® as the foundation that sends kids to Disney World. The work seemed simple enough—plane tickets, hotel accommodations, gate passes for the family. The children are given the opportunity to meet Mickey, their "truest friend," as one of the poems describes him. After the weekend, the family returns home with a photo album of souvenirs.

But that's not the end of the story. The Make-A-Wish® Kids have more friends than even they realize. This book testifies to that fact. In addition to the volunteers in the photos, a host of poets, essay writers, photographers, book designers, graphic artists, publishers, publicists, and even musicians (the list could go on) have come together to produce something much larger than a souvenir photo album. *The Eyes of a Wish*™ celebrates a community where selflessness and dedication are the keys to entry, where hope is the buzzword, and where children feel at home.

The Eyes of Wish™ is the beginning of a compelling story. Get to know the characters. Pass the book around. Stories are meant to be told, and this one is interactive—there's plenty of room for additional characters, more and more "truest friends."

Kenny and his mom Laura

Wade Caldwell

ACKNOWLEDGMENTS

The Eyes of a Wish would not have been possible without the efforts and dedication of four very special groups: the wish children and their families, a devoted group of volunteers, the staff of Make-A-Wish Foundation® of Greater Atlanta & North Georgia, and the underwriters. This book was truly an inspired team effort that exemplifies what a small group can accomplish when everyone works together.

I thank the wish children and their families who saw the potential to help other children with life-threatening illnesses participate in the magic of having a wish granted by Make-A-Wish Foundation® The wish families' unselfish support and enthusiasm for this project was a constant source of love and inspiration for everyone who worked on this book.

I thank the volunteers who contributed their time and efforts, including the many writers and photographers who are not listed on the previous pages. There were many volunteers who provided the support, input, advice, and coordination that made the inaugural effort of *The Eyes of a Wish* a success. They are LiAn Chapman, Janis Hiett, Kerry Parker, Cara Chotiner, Rachel Weinstein, Joanne Wesloske, Emily Johnson, Kathy Gamble, Karen Strott, and Becky Mazon. The Atlanta Symphony Orchestra provided valuable promotional assistance in the early stages of the project. I thank Lizanne Nichols, Mary Wilson, and Allison Vulgamore for helping us get the word out about the book. I thank Preston Merchant, who agreed to edit this book when it was only an idea. His readiness to lend his expertise and talents after a brief explanation over the phone is testament both to the power of Make-A-Wish® and to the values Sewanee instilled in both of us.

I thank the staff of the Greater Atlanta & North Georgia chapter, whose wish children were photographed for this book; all the staff worked very hard to make it a success. Diane Valek and Stephanie Nelson saw potential in this project from a brief outline and provided invaluable support and direction. I extend special thanks to Helen Shepard. Without her tireless dedication to and love for the Make-A-Wish® kids coupled with her ability to get things done, this project would not have captured the range of expression and emotion that is Make-A-Wish®. I thank Jim Grant and Wendy Roberts from the project's advisory committee for their sage advice, inspiration, and support.

The Eyes of a Wish would not have taken shape without the companies and individuals who when asked to contribute responded with their hearts. I thank all who contributed time, money, and services. I extend special thanks to the first to become involved in the project, Laura Tallman from Agfa and Keith Sequera and the entire crew at Focus Atlanta. Their support was immediate and enthusiastic, even when all I had to show them was an idea. Without the photographic advice of Dale, Robert, and Barry, the images the photographers captured would never have reproduced so well. I thank David Womick and the crew at Earthling Films for filming and producing the promotional video and public service announcements for *The Eyes of a Wish*.

COLOPHON

The more than 3,000 images that were taken for this book were captured on Agfa professional films that were developed by Focus Atlanta. The final images were printed on Agfa paper that was donated by Agfa Division of Bayer Corporation. The text was typeset in Trajan and Granjon. The text was printed on 100# Signature Satin Text that was donated by Zellerbach and Mead Papers at Action Digital Color in Atlanta, Georgia. The images were printed as 175-line elliptical dot duotones in high-density black and warm grey. The book was smythe sewn and bound at Nicholstone in Nashville, Tennessee.